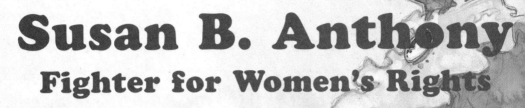

Susan B. Anthony
Fighter for Women's Rights

written by
Deborah Hopkinson

illustrated by
Amy Bates

USE YOUR VOTE

OTES FOR WOMEN

Ready-to-Read • Aladdin
New York   London   Toronto   Sydney

For my niece, Haley Fairbrother,
who shares Susan's birthday—and her spirit.
—D. H.

To my grandma, mother, and sisters.
—A. B.

ALADDIN PAPERBACKS

An imprint of Simon & Schuster Children's Publishing Division

1230 Avenue of the Americas, New York, NY 10020

Text copyright © 2005 by Deborah Hopkinson

Illustrations copyright © 2005 by Amy Bates

ALADDIN PAPERBACKS and colophon are trademarks of
Simon & Schuster, Inc.

READY-TO-READ is a registered trademark of Simon & Schuster, Inc.

Also available in an Aladdin Library edition.

Designed by Lisa Vega

The text of this book was set in CenturyOldst BT.

Manufactured in the United States of America

First Aladdin Paperbacks edition November 2005

2 4 6 8 10 9 7 5 3 1

Library of Congress Cataloging-in-Publication Data

Hopkinson, Deborah.

Susan B. Anthony : fighter for women's rights / by Deborah Hopkinson ;

illustrated by Amy Bates.—1st Aladdin Paperbacks ed.

p. cm. — (Ready-to-read stories of famous Americans)

ISBN-13: 978-0-689-86909-9 (pbk.)   ISBN-10: 0-689-86909-6 (pbk.)

ISBN-13: 978-0-689-86910-5 (library ed.)   ISBN-10: 0-689-86910-X (library ed.)

1. Anthony, Susan B. (Susan Brownell), 1820-1906—Juvenile literature.

2. Feminists—United States—Biography—Juvenile literature. 3. Suffragists—

United States—Biography—Juvenile literature. 4. Women social

reformers—United States—Biography—Juvenile literature. 5. Women's rights—

United States—History—Juvenile literature. I. Bates, Amy June. II. Title. III. Series.

HQ1413.A55H67 2005

305.42'092—dc22   2004031074

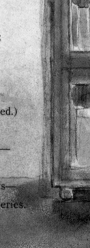

Susan B. Anthony
Fighter for Women's Rights

Failure is impossible.
—Susan B. Anthony, 1906

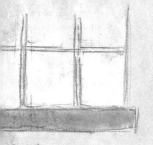

Chapter 1
A Hardworking Girl

Susan B. Anthony was born in 1820. When Susan lived, not all people in America had the right to live and work as they pleased.

Some people were slaves, with no rights at all. Women didn't have many rights either. Married women couldn't own land. Girls couldn't go to college. No woman was allowed to vote.

Susan wanted to *reform*, or change, America. She believed American women should have the right to vote, just as men did. With her friend Elizabeth Cady Stanton, Susan spent her life fighting for women's rights. But the fight to win the vote took longer than Susan ever imagined.

Susan Brownell Anthony was born in Massachusetts. Her father, Daniel, was a Quaker. He believed in a simple life of hard work.

Susan's father owned a mill where young women wove cotton into cloth. Eleven of the mill girls lived with Susan's big family.

Susan and her sisters helped their mother cook and clean for all these people. It took all day to bake twenty loaves of bread!

Unlike many people at that time, Susan's father believed girls should get an education.

Susan learned to read when she was only four. But long hours reading books in poor light hurt her eyes. Susan's right eye became crossed because of reading in poor light, and stayed that way her whole life.

Even so, Susan loved learning. Sometimes she went to school. Other times she was taught at home.

When Susan was eleven, she asked her father to make a young woman the boss of the other workers in the mill because Susan could see the woman knew more than the boss, who was a man.

Susan's father said no. Although he thought women and men were equal, he wasn't ready to change how things were done. And in those days a man was always the boss.

Susan loved her father, but she couldn't understand his decision. Why *shouldn't* a woman be the boss? Why *not* start changing the world?

Susan began asking hard questions like these when she was a young girl, and she never stopped.

When Susan was in her teens, hard times hit. Her father lost his mill, and even their house.

To help out, Susan became a teacher at a boarding school. She missed her family very much.

Soon, though, Susan got used to being on her own. She did well and became a head teacher. Although Susan had boyfriends, in the end she chose not to marry. She didn't want to give up her freedom.

After ten years of teaching, Susan was ready to take on new challenges. Somehow, Susan wanted to help make America a better place. But what could one woman do?

O Slavery, hateful thing . . .
—Susan B. Anthony, 1854

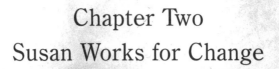

Chapter Two
Susan Works for Change

Susan was almost thirty when she went home to live on her family's new farm near Rochester, New York.

At first, Susan spent time helping out on the family farm. But soon she was spending most of her time with other people like herself, who wanted to reform America.

It was just like Susan to rush off to an important meeting and forget to water the raspberries!

Many of Susan's new friends were
abolitionists, people who wanted to
abolish, or end, slavery.

Susan and her family became part
of the Underground Railroad, a group of
people who helped runaway slaves
escape north to Canada and freedom.
Susan's home became a gathering place
for abolitionists.

Then, in 1851, Susan visited the town of Seneca Falls, New York. There, on a street corner, she was introduced to Elizabeth Cady Stanton.

Susan was excited to meet Mrs. Stanton. Mrs. Stanton was already famous for her work for women's rights.

Susan knew that Mrs. Stanton, along with Lucretia Mott, had organized the first women's rights convention in July of 1848.

At this meeting Mrs. Stanton had declared that women were equal with men. She said married women should be able to own property. Most important of all, Mrs. Stanton believed women should have the right to vote!

Just about everyone thought Elizabeth Cady Stanton was foolish to demand the vote for American women. But Susan agreed with Mrs. Stanton. She realized that unless women could vote, own property, and be full citizens, they'd never have power over their own lives, or equal rights with men.

WOMAN'S RIGHTS CONVENTION

SENECA FALLS, NY, JULY 19, 20, 1848

The true woman . . . will be her own individual self.
—Susan B. Anthony, 1857

Chapter Three
Friend and Fighter

Before long Susan and Mrs. Stanton became close friends and leaders of the fight for women's rights.

Since Mrs. Stanton often had to stay home with her small children, it was up to Susan to spread the word.

Susan set out to bring the message about women's rights to people all over New York State. Susan B. Anthony had found her true work.

Susan spent long hours on the road. She traveled alone by train or carriage. Sometimes she braved snowstorms in an open sleigh.

To help pay her way, Susan charged twenty-five cents for her speeches. Sometimes hundreds of people came to hear her speak. Other times only a few showed up.

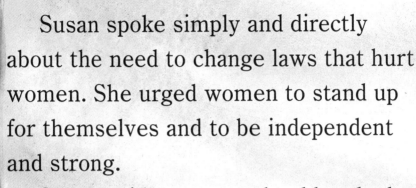

Susan spoke simply and directly about the need to change laws that hurt women. She urged women to stand up for themselves and to be independent and strong.

Susan said a woman should make her own choices, do her own work, and stand on her own feet. And that's exactly what Susan B. Anthony herself was doing.

We shall simply have to work on . . .
—Susan B. Anthony, 1903

Chapter Four
The Right to Vote

Along with speaking out for women, Susan also worked with abolitionists to end slavery.

The abolitionist men had one goal: to free enslaved people. They were glad to have Susan fight for their cause. But they didn't want to fight for women's rights.

In 1861 the Civil War began. During the war all anyone could think about was the struggle between North and South.

But in 1865 the Civil War ended. Once the slaves were free, Susan hoped that all Americans, white and black, men and women, would gain the right to vote.

In 1865 Congress passed the Fourteenth Amendment to the U.S. Constitution. This gave voting rights to former slaves—but *only* to men. All women, black and white, would have to wait.

Many women, including Susan, Mrs. Stanton, and Sojourner Truth, a former slave herself, were angry and upset about this. Yet they had no choice: They had to keep on fighting.

Susan and Mrs. Stanton traveled from state to state, speaking out for women's suffrage—the right to vote. They also formed the National Woman Suffrage Association.

Working to change laws and the way people thought was hard. Even the women who cared most about equal rights couldn't always agree on the best way to get America to change. But Susan never gave up.

My natural rights, my civil rights . . . are all ignored.
—Susan B. Anthony, 1873

Chapter Five
Failure Is Impossible

In 1872 Susan put America's laws to the test. On Election Day she and more than one hundred women across the nation went to the polls to cast their votes.

"Well, I have been and gone and done it!" Susan wrote to her dear friend Mrs. Stanton.

Just as she expected, Susan was arrested. She didn't go to jail, but she was put on trial. The judge found her guilty. When he asked Susan if she had anything to say, she leaped to her feet and gave a daring speech. But it was no use.

On July 4, 1876, America turned one hundred. In a celebration in Philadelphia the Declaration of Independence was read. At the end, to everyone's surprise, Susan got up and handed out a new declaration—a Declaration of Rights for Women.

Susan and other women took their fight to the Congress. Beginning in 1887 Congress looked at changing the U.S. Constitution to give women the vote. But year after year, Congress said no.

In February of 1906 Susan B. Anthony turned eighty-six. Her dear friend Mrs. Stanton had died a few years earlier. Susan attended her last women's rights meeting, helping to raise money for the future.

When it was time for Susan's last speech, she struggled to her feet as the audience applauded.

Susan's voice rang out clear. She urged women not to give up. "Failure is impossible!" she cried.

Susan B. Anthony died just a few weeks later. It took American women another fourteen years—until 1920—to win the right to vote.

If I could only live another century!
—Susan B. Anthony, 1902

Here is a time line of the life of Susan B. Anthony:

1820   Susan Brownell Anthony is born in Adams, Massachusetts, on February 15.

1848   The first women's rights convention is held in Seneca Falls, New York.

1851   Susan and Elizabeth Cady Stanton meet and become friends.

1852   Susan attends her first women's rights convention in Syracuse, New York.

1854   Susan begins to travel in New York to get support for women's rights.

1856   Susan becomes a speaker for the American Anti-Slavery Society.

1861   The Civil War begins.

1868   The Fourteenth Amendment grants the right to vote to black males.

1872   Susan is arrested for voting and is brought to trial in June of the next year.

1887   The Sixteenth Amendment, women's right to vote, is first voted down by the U.S. Senate.

1906   Susan gives her "Failure Is Impossible" speech; she dies on March 13, at age eighty-six.

1920   The Nineteenth Amendment grants women the right to vote.

1979   The Susan B. Anthony dollar coin is introduced.